Hats and Caps

By Debbie Croft

Sam is in the pit.

Sam has a hat and a pin.

hat

pin

pit

Tim has a cap.

The cap fits.

Tim bats in his cap.

Hit, Tim, hit!

cap

bat

Pen is at the tap.

Pen has a hat.

The hat has a rim.

It is Bec.

Bec has a cap.

Bec is fit!

cap

CHECKING FOR MEANING

1. Who is in the pit? *(Literal)*

2. What does Tim do in his cap? *(Literal)*

3. Why do you think Pen is at the tap? *(Inferential)*

EXTENDING VOCABULARY

pit	What is the meaning of *pit* in this book? What other pits do you know of?
pin	Find the word *pin* in the book. Change the letter *i* to an *e* and read the new word.
cap	A *cap* is worn on your head. What other words describe things you can wear on your head?

MOVING BEYOND THE TEXT

1. Why does each person have a different hat or cap?

2. What are some reasons other people wear hats or caps? Are all their hats and caps the same? Why or why not?

3. Who wears a hat as part of their uniform? How are these hats different?

4. What different materials are hats made from? Where can you buy different types of hats?

SPEED SOUNDS

Cc	Bb	Rr	Ee	Ff	Hh	Nn
Mm	Ss	Aa	Pp	Ii	Tt	

PRACTICE WORDS

in

hat

pin

bats

cap

fits

hit

bat

Hit

Pen

Bec

rim

fit